Tota pulchra es

"Tota pulchra es" is a fourth-century prayer based on texts from the books of Judith and Song of Songs. It is used liturgically in the Second Vespers for the Feast of the Immaculate Conception.

Tota pulchra es, Maria,
et macula originalis non est in te.
Vestimentum tuum candidum quasi nix,
et facies tua sicut sol.
Tota pulchra es, Maria,
et macula originalis non est in te.
Tu gloria Jerusalem,
tu laetitia Israel,
tu honorificentia populi nostri.
Tota pulchra es, Maria.

You are beautiful, Maria,
and the original stain is not in you.
Your clothing is as white as snow,
and your face is like the sun.
You are beautiful, Maria,
and the original stain is not in you.
You are the glory of Jerusalem,
you are the joy of Israel,
you are the honor of our people.
You are beautiful, Maria.

Tu es Petrus

In Matthew 16:18–19 Jesus gives his disciple Simon the name Peter (Petrus), which means "rock" in Latin. Peter is recognized as the first Pope, interpreting the metaphor of being handed the "keys of the kingdom" as a sacred charge to be God's representative on earth. Duruflé set only the first half of verse 18. Other musical settings of this text often include both verses 18 and 19.

Tu es Petrus
et super hanc petram aedificabo Ecclesiam meam.

You are Peter
and upon this rock I will build my church.

Tantum ergo

The text of "Tantum ergo" is the penultimate stanza of "Pange Lingua Gloriosi" by St. Thomas Aquinas (1225–1274). In some traditional Masses this text is used during the veneration and benediction of the Blessed Sacrament.

Tantum ergo Sacramentum
Veneremur cernui,
Et antiquum documentum
Novo cedat ritui,
Praestet fides supplementum
Sensuum defectui.

Genitori, genitoque
Laus et jubilatio,
Salus, honor, virtus quoque
Sit et benedictio,
Procedenti ab utroque
Comparsit laudation.
Amen.

Therefore, so great a sacrament
Let us worship with bowed heads
And may the ancient practice
give way to the new rite;
May faith supply a substitute
for the failure of the senses.

To the begetter and the begotton
be praise and jubilation,
Hail, honor, virtue also,
And blessing.
To the one proceeding from both
Let there be equal praise.
Amen.

Quatre Motets
sur des thèmes grégoriens,
Op. 10

Maurice Duruflé
(1902–1986)

For mixed chorus a cappella.

Composed: 1960

First known performance: 4 May 1961, Église Saint-Merri, Paris, Chorale Stéphane Caillat.

Duration: approximately 8 minutes

Duruflé grew up in Louviers in the northern French region of Haute-Normandie (Upper Normandy), where as a boy he was a chorister and studied piano. At the age of 17 he moved to Paris to study organ with Charles Tournemire. A year later Duruflé was admitted to the Paris Conservatoire, where he studied organ, piano and composition, and was awarded five first prizes in various subjects. Upon graduation Duruflé became musical assistant to Louis Vierne at Notre Dame, but soon after this was appointed organist at Saint Étienne-du-Mont in Paris, where he would remain for the rest of his life. In 1943 he was appointed professor of harmony at the Conservatoire, a position he maintained for 27 years. From 1926 until 1977 Duruflé published 14 compositions, including the Requiem, Op. 9 (1947). Duruflé traveled extensively as a concert organist, and was active as a recording artist. Later in life he and his second wife often performed as an organ duo. The composer suffered severe injuries in an automobile accident in 1975, which left him nearly bed-ridden for the final decade of his life.

Composed in 1960, *Quatre Motets sur des thèmes grégoriens*, Op. 10 (Four Motets on Gregorian Themes) were dedicated to Auguste le Guennant, director of the Gregorian Institute in Paris. Each of the four motets begins with an incipit of Gregorian chant, which serves as melodic inspiration for the composition that follows.

Ubi caritas
"Ubi caritas" is an early Christian antiphon traditionally used in the Maundy Thursday service during the washing of the feet, an act of Jesus from the Last Supper. The antiphon has become closely associated with the Eucharist, and is sometimes also used at weddings. Duruflé sets only the first of the four stanzas of the text.

Ubi caritas et amor, Deus ibi est.	Where charity and love are, God is there.
Congregavit nos in unum Christi amor.	Christ's love has gathered us into one.
Exsultemus et in ipso jucundemur.	Let us rejoice and be pleased in Him.
Timeamus et amemus Deum vivum.	Let us fear, and let us love the living God.
Et ex corde diligamus nos sincero.	And may we love each other with a sincere heart.
Amen.	Amen.

50565708

$10.99

MAURICE DURUFLÉ
Quatre Motets sur des thèmes grégoriens, Op. 10

FRENCH CHORAL MASTERS

DURAND

à Auguste le Guennant,
directeur de l'Institut grégorien de Paris

I. UBI CARITAS

for four-part mixed chorus
(with two alternating alto parts)

Ubi cári.tas et ámor, Dé.us i.bi est.

Maurice Duruflé
Op. 10

© 1960 Éditions DURAND
Paris, France

8

12

16

(Altos un peu en dehors jusqu'à "Ubi caritas")

-mus et in íp - so___ ju-cun dé - mur. Ti-me-á - mus

-té-mus et in íp - so___ ju-cun dé - mur. Ti-me-á - mus

-té-mus et in íp - so ju-cun dé - mur. Ti-me-á - mus

-té-mus et in íp - so ju-cun dé - mur. Ti-me-á - mus

20

et a - mé-mus Dé - um ví - vum. Et ex cór - de di - li -

et a - mé-mus Dé - um ví - vum. Et ex cór - de di - li -

et a - mé-mus Dé - um ví - vum. Et ex cór - de di - li -

et a - mé-mus Dé - um ví - vum. Et ex cór - de di - li -

23

-gá-mus nos sin - cé - ro. Et ex cór-de di - li - gá mus nos sin -
-gá-mus nos _ sin - cé - ro. Et ex cór-de di - li - gá mus nos _ sin -
-gá-mus nos sin - cé - ro. Et ex cór-de di - li - gá mus nos sin -
-gá-mus nos sin - cé - ro. Et ex cór-de di - li - gá mus nos sin -

27

poco ced. **Tempo**

-cé - ro, sin - cé - ro.
-cé - ro. U - bi cá - ri - tas et á -
-cé - ro, sin - cé - ro. U - bi cá - ri - tas et á -
-cé - ro, sin - cé - ro. U - bi cá - ri - tas et á -

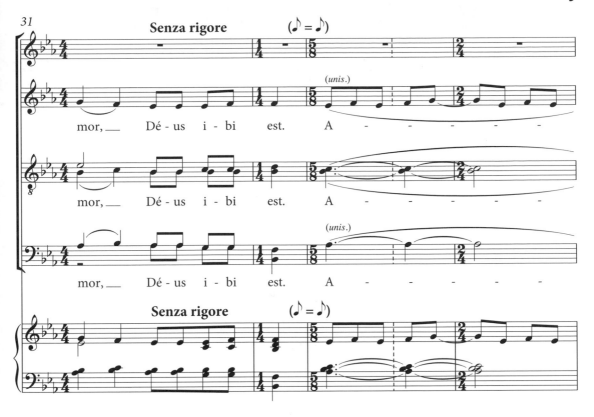

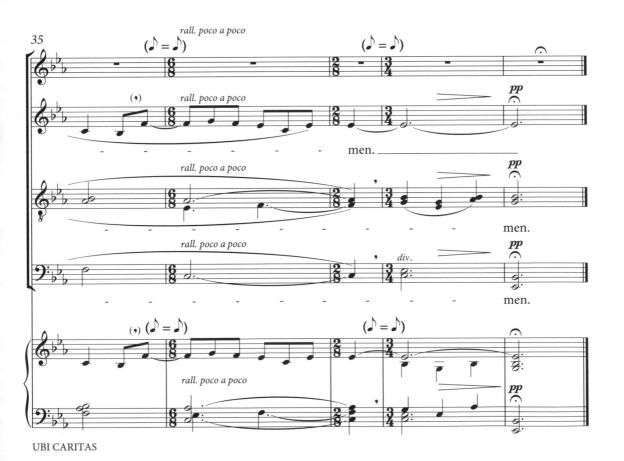

II. TOTA PULCHRA ES

for three-part women's chorus

Tóta púlchra es Mari_a

Maurice Duruflé
Op. 10

TOTA PULCHRA ES

17

nix, _____ et fá - ci - es __ tú - a sic - ut sol, __ sic - ut

qua - si nix, et fá - ci - es __ tú - a sic - ut sol, __ sic - ut

qua - si nix, et fá - ci - es tú - a sic - ut sol, __ sic - ut

21

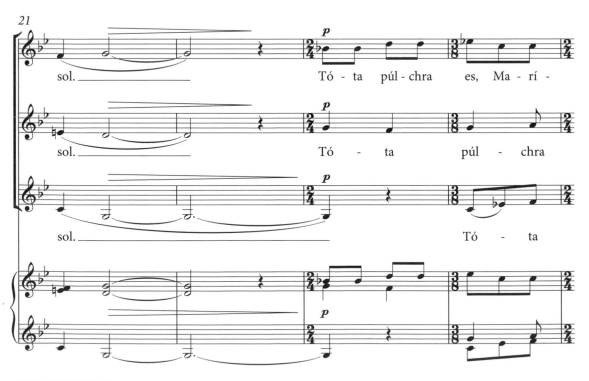

sol. _____ Tó - ta púl - chra es, Ma - rí -

sol. _____ Tó - ta púl - chra

sol. _____ Tó - ta

33

37

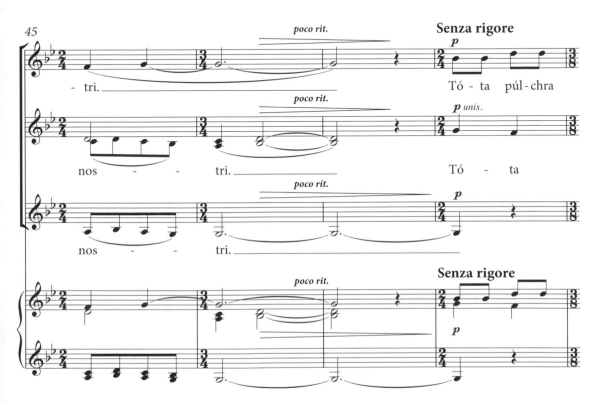

TOTA PULCHRA ES

49

es, Ma - rí - a, _____ tó - ta púl - chra es, Ma - rí -

púl - chra es, Ma - rí - a, tó - ta púl - chra

Tó - ta púl - chra es, tó - ta _____ púl - chra

53

-a. _____ Ma - rí - a.

es, Ma - rí - a, _____ Ma - ri - a.

es, _____ Ma - ri - a.

III. TU ES PETRUS
for four-part mixed chorus

Maurice Duruflé
Op. 10

© 1960 Éditions DURAND
Paris, France

TU ES PETRUS

TU ES PETRUS

IV. TANTUM ERGO

for four-part mixed chorus

Maurice Duruflé
Op. 10

© 1960 Éditions DURAND
Paris, France

TANTUM ERGO

TANTUM ERGO

ISBN 978-1-4803-1269-2

9 781480 312692

TANTUM ERGO